CONNECTION POINTS
FOR
Life

DAILY
<u>DEVOTIONAL</u>
SIMPLE TRUTHS THAT
CONNECT TO GOD'S PURPOSE

V. ROCHELLE RICHARDSON

Copyright © 2023 V. Rochelle Richardson
All Rights Reserved

Table of Contents

Dedication v

Preface vi

It's Just A Setup! There's Victory In The Wait! 1

Father, Let Me Hear You. 4

Come Up Higher! 8

You Call That Love? 13

He Loved Me Till The End. 19

He Really Will Wipe Your Tears Away. 24

God Owns The "When." 29

True Victory Starts With Knowing Who You Are. 35

Can Anybody Tell Me How Long Do I Have To Wait? 43

Divine Connections 50

Dedication

I want to dedicate this book to my children Delisa, Halbert Jr. and Christina. It has been said that it is our job to teach, mentor and rear our children. But through life, I've learned so much as I've watched you grow into the healthy, responsible adults that you are. You often share things you've learned from me through the years. And I think to myself, "if only you knew." I stumbled through so much with each of you. Thank you for letting me practice. When I look at you three, something inside of me says, I did something right. I'm glad I'm your mama!

Preface

I knew as a child that my life was not just ordinary. From one tragedy to the next. From one disappointment to the next. Of course I'm no different from anyone else. All of us have challenges and struggles. But it's how we navigate through them all that gets us through. In this book God showed me how everything I went through in life was somehow connected to my destiny. I remember hearing Him whisper those very words to my ear one day. It didn't make sense then and sometimes even now it doesn't make sense. But thank God He shows us how to connect those challenges in a way that will not only benefit you but those who will take the time to read. I pray that's what this devotional book will do for you.

You may think your life is full of twists and turns and none of it makes sense. Yet your Heavenly Father has a plan that will work for your good.

Make sure to get the understanding about the thing, connect it to your now, and watch God be God in your life.

It's Just A Setup!
There's Victory In The Wait!

Genesis 50:20 NIV

"You intended to harm me, but God intended it for good to accomplish what is now being done, the saving of many lives."

Joseph was his father's favorite son, which caused his brothers to hate him. You know how it is if you happen to be that favorite child. To the parents, that child can do nothing wrong, but to your siblings you are everything but right. That child gets to choose where the family eats when they go out. That child seemingly has less chores than the rest of the crew and even then, your mom wants you to pitch in to help them. Now, I'm not talking about myself; I just "heard" that's how it is sometimes. Okay, back to Joseph. Not only was he the favorite child, he also had the nerve to have a dream that depicts his family bowing down to him. Narrating his dreams to them made them hate him even more, to the point that they planned to kill him. Instead of killing him, they staged his death and sold him into slavery.

After being sold into slavery and put in prison for a crime he didn't commit, he made good use of his time. While in prison, he continued to interpret dreams of his fellow prisoners, including one who served as the cupbearer to Pharoah. Favor! It was a *setup!*

> *Just when you thought things were working out for your good, here comes the enemy. His work comes mainly through people you know. They seem to have the blueprint for your life. Although you understand that God speaks to you as well. When you don't give in to their plans, they devise a plan to destroy you. Take heart in Joseph's story. The enemy's plan will not work when God's plan is already at work.*

PRAYER

Father, I place my entire life in your hands. I submit to your will only. Help me to trust your plan even when those around me want to harm me. I declare victory in the face of it all. In Jesus Name. Amen!

Connection Points For Life

My connection point:

Father, Let Me Hear You.

Habakkuk 2:1 NIV

"I will stand at my watch and station myself on the ramparts; I will look to see what He will say to me, and what answer I am to give to this complaint."

Habakkuk's declaration here to "stand" and "station" himself to hear what The Lord has to say was not as loyal and easy as it sounds. He had prayed for an answer and seemingly God hadn't responded, or so he thought. Then he went to accuse God of not hearing him. He was praying for the rescue of God's people. He lamented in chapter 1:2 "Oh Lord, how long shall I cry for help, and you will not listen?" The Lord finally responds but His response was, "keep waiting, be patient." He tells Habakkuk that He's sending the Babylonians but doesn't give any specifics as to when. In Habakkuk 1:5, He simply said, "I'm going to do something amazing in your days." Does that sound remotely familiar? I know I've had many petitions before The Lord, and as I sit to wait, He speaks and simply says, "I hear you." The next question that I seldom ask is, "Okay, can You answer?" As I grew stronger in my Christian journey, I discovered a few things while waiting.

God changes:

- **My pride to humility (I'm not in charge after all).**
- **Doubt into faith and peace.**
- **My intimacy in The Lord grows.**

It's funny how we stay by the phone while waiting on an important call. Wait in line for groceries and nine months for the baby to arrive. But when we pray and petition God, we need answers now!

You may be waiting for an answer to a specific problem, and it seems as though nothing is happening. While Habakkuk grew impatient, we can still learn a valuable lesson here. While waiting on The Lord to answer, Habakkuk didn't seek any alternative means to get answers. He postured himself, militant style, and simply waited. A watchman must rid himself of all distractions to fully concentrate on the task of protecting the city. Habakkuk took his eyes off his circumstances and focused on God for an answer and move. After that, he became confident and expectant that God sees and will certainly move. Many of us are eager to hear from God, but we want Him to speak the way we want. Let us free ourselves from the burden of trying to "make" things happen. I'm learning to listen to whoever and whatever God chooses to use to speak to me. Be it a child, a road sign, the clerk at the store, your boss, your enemy, the mechanic, the maintenance person, whoever and whatever. We position ourselves to hear and hearken to Your voice Lord.

PRAYER

God, *You are Mighty and Great. I know You are with me because You promised. You brought me this far and You will not forsake me now. I bow before You in humble submission. Remove all anxiousness from my mind. Speak Lord, for Your servant heareth. I will wait patiently on You for guidance, wisdom and instructions. In Jesus Name. Amen!*

Connection Points For Life

My connection point:

Come Up Higher!

Isaiah 55:8-9 NIV

"For my thoughts are not your thoughts, neither are your ways my ways," declares the Lord. "As the heavens are higher than the earth, so are my ways higher than your ways and my thoughts than your thoughts."

Have you ever tried to get something from the top shelf? Be it in your house or the grocery store. I tried to help a lady the other day with a top shelf item at a local store. I'm not extremely tall but I was taller than she was. I was quite proud of myself as I asked her "do you need some help?" To which she immediately replied, "Yes Please." I pushed my cart out of the way, asked her which item she wanted, and proceeded to reach for it. Well, at 66 years of age, I assume that I've had some shrinkage in the height department. Because I could touch the item, but I couldn't grip it to pull it down. I stood back, regrouped and went for it again. But still I was only able to touch it without taking hold of it. All of a sudden, we both heard a voice saying, "You need some help?" We turned to see a guy shorter than both of us. But what made the difference was that he had a ladder in his hand. Then we discovered he was a worker at the store. He put the ladder in place, climbed up and retrieved the item with ease. He was only able to achieve the goal because he had the necessary tool to go higher; a ladder. In his own ability, we both would have laughed at him offering us help when he was shorter than the both of us.

There are things Our Father wants to share with us, but we can't hear Him because we haven't taken the steps to come up higher in our walk with Him. We may believe we have the answers but if we're living a mediocre Christian lifestyle, we absolutely cannot comprehend God's Ways and Thoughts.

My family, for the most part, are football fanatics. To the point that after Superbowl Sunday, they really don't have any interest in watching television until the next football season. They were introduced to the game at a young age. They studied it. They know all the players and the plays. They can often call what the referees will say before they say it. On the other hand, I truly don't understand it, so I'm not totally disappointed when the season ends.

Here's the thing; the time they have spent learning the game is the reason they know it so well. What is it with us believers that makes us feel we can spend little time with God yet we expect Him to do big things for us?

When we spend time with God, we get a greater insight as to who He is and what He did before. Even though we may have no idea of how or what He's going to do about a matter, but knowing Him and His Word helps to build us up. My personal experience is that when I spend time with The Lord, my senses and sensitivity becomes sharper. God's Word just rolls out my mouth without forethought. It's a great feeling to know you are so connected to Our Father that you wait on His every Word.

As we press into Him, our level of confidence grows. No matter the trial that comes our way, we are assured victory when we stay in His presence. Because that's who He is.

It must have been around 2005-2006 that I was attacked in my body. I had an emergency surgery to get relief since the pain was so bad. Following the surgery, I noticed I was very short of breath when I tried to talk. My doctor placed me on a high level of oxygen to assist me, but still I was winded to the point that I couldn't speak without gasping for breath. I finally got to the point where I stopped trying to talk and I began writing notes to everyone about what I needed. I had just truly started developing my relationship with The Lord in prayer and I remember being very sad that I couldn't open my mouth to pray. Over the night, I heard The Lord whisper to my spirit

"You know I can hear your thoughts afar off, right?" I literally responded in my head "yeah, but...." At that moment, He said, "Well, talk to me." Now, mind you that I never opened my mouth when He asked me the question, but He responded so very quickly and it took me by surprise. Let me tell you, those next few days of my non-verbal communication were the best days of my life with The Lord. I would ask a question, with my mind, and He would respond. And when I entered a mode of worship, I literally felt Angels glorifying God with me. These are the things that will transpire as we come up higher in Him. Acts 17:*28 NIV "For in Him we live and move and have our being.' As some of your own poets have said, 'We are His offspring.'*

PRAYER

Father, *it is my utmost desire to be in Your Presence. You are my Joy. You are my Peace. You are my Protector. I hunger after You and because I do, You feed me with Manna from on high. Bring me even closer to You Dear Jesus. In Jesus Name. Amen!*

Connection Points For Life

My connection point:

You Call That Love?

Romans 5:3-5 NIV

"We can rejoice, too, when we run into problems and trials, for we know that they help us develop endurance. And endurance develops strength of character, and character strengthens our confident hope of salvation. And this hope will not lead to disappointment. For we know how dearly God loves us, because He has given us the Holy Spirit to fill our hearts with His love."

I may be the only one who feels this way sometimes, but I don't think so. Have you ever felt so far from The Lord? I especially feel this when I'm going through a trial. Life can just come at you from every direction at one time and you find yourself helpless as to where to turn. Our first thought should always be to Our Father, who knows it all. But sadly, we don't always go to Him first. Hopefully, eventually, but not at first. When we don't go to Him first, it makes us question His love for us.

I remember the year was 1969. Boy, what a year! My 40-year-old mother was battling a vicious kidney disease, and the only way she was going to survive was to receive a kidney transplant. Now, transplants of any kind in those days were not as popular as they are now in recent years. So, finding a matching donor was pretty challenging. My 19-year-old brother, who was in the military serving in Vietnam at the time, got wind of it and decided to see if he was a match. We finally got word that yes, he was a match for our mother. Although mom was not overly excited to have her son donate a kidney, she agreed to it because at this point, it was the only way she was going to survive.

The Red Cross got him home expeditiously because time was running out for mom. He arrived home to Detroit on Thursday, September 25th. The transplant was to take place on Monday, September 29th. So, my brother had a couple of days to see some of his friends before the big operation. Back then, being in the military was such an honorable assignment. You were greatly esteemed for your service. It should still be that way, but I digress. Meanwhile, at 13 years old, I was very busy getting my mother's suitcase prepared for the hospital. I was the youngest and the only girl, and I didn't have any problems trying to help take care of my mother. She was my world. I did everything I could do to ease her worries and I did it gladly; I washed her clothes daily, prepared her meals, and I helped her get dressed daily. In addition to taking care of mom, I still made my own arrangements to get to church every

Sunday. On this particular weekend, I asked my father to take me, and he agreed.

Everything was set. Mom's dinner was prepared. My clothes for church were laid out. My choir robe was pressed. I felt proud of myself. As I prepared to get in bed, the telephone rang. My brother, Michael, answered it and called me to the phone. He said it was our dad. My first thought was, "Oh boy, he's changed his mind about taking me to church." I answered the phone with a little attitude, "Yes, daddy." All I could hear was someone on the other end sniffling. I said it again "Yes, daddy." Still nothing. Before I could say the next word, my father blurted out "Kenny is dead." You can imagine every horrifying thought that rushed through my head. "Was this some sort of joke?" This was not supposed to happen. Kenny came home to donate a kidney to my mother. Without it she had little to no chance of surviving. Disbelief! Fear! Troubled! What now? Were the things whirling around my head. My beautiful 19-year-old brother, Kenneth David Scruggs, who was the most personable person you ever wanted to meet was gone. A robbery gone bad that resulted in a senseless murder. I understood the severity of the matter but for a 13-year-old, not everything registered to me. I definitely didn't realize that my mom would soon transition without the kidney transplant. I guess I didn't think it was permanent. But I soon found out.

We buried my brother, Kenny, on October 4, 1969 and my sweet beautiful mom on December 20, 1969. In a span of about 2 months, two people that I loved with my entire being was gone. All I could think of was, "You call this love?" How could a God that I served all my young life allow these things to happen? What did I do that was so bad that He would take my loved ones away? All I had was my mom. You know the phrase 'attached to the hip?' That was me! Where she went, I went. Even before she became ill, I would rush home after school just to sit and talk with her. I never imagined my life without my mom. But here I am, standing at her graveside. Jesus! This can't be real. But it surely was. I had thoughts of jumping in the hole and going with her, but then another thought came to me that I wouldn't be dead, just maybe get a broken leg out of the deal. Suddenly, I heard a whisper, "I'll never leave you nor forsake you!" I have never heard those words before. Now, I know you're thinking I thought she was a church girl. Well, I was. I went to church every Sunday, sang in the choir, became the Sunday School secretary, participated in all church events whether it be plays or raffles, Bible drills, you name it, I did it all. Sadly enough, I was a church girl but the church wasn't in me. Oh, I had the fear of The Lord, hence, I didn't participate in anything that I thought would displease The Lord. But I really didn't know Him. At the moment of that whisper however, I felt a peace come over me. I didn't know how, but I knew at that moment that God was going to take care of me.

I can't explain the year 1969. But I can say that from that time to this very moment, God has taken really good care of me. Thank You My Father. I can't say that I ever got the answers to "You call this love?" But what I did get in exchange was God's Peace.

PRAYER

Heavenly Father, for my brother or sister that's reading this passage right now, please envelope them in Your Loving Arms. Some of them feel what I felt all those years ago and are asking, "How can a God that loves me allow these things to happen?" We may never get an answer in the living, but what we do know is that, despite what it is, You promised to never leave or forsake us. We can trust that. We can rely on that because we know that you are able to fulfill your promises. So, we relish in Your loving embrace as we continue to navigate through waters that are not always clear. But You're right there to lead and guide us through it all. In Jesus Name. Amen!

Connection Points For Life

My connection point:

He Loved Me Till The End.

John 13:1 NIV

"...He loved them to the end."

My beloved husband of 40 years went to be with Jesus on December 23, 2015. He was everything I could've ever wanted in a husband. We married at the ripe ages of 18 (me) and 20 (him). Three beautiful children came out of this perfectly imperfect marriage. To say we were proud is an understatement. Since we were still very young, we made a lot of mistakes. Neither of us had a pattern for a godly marriage, so we had to fish our way through the terrains of life. I can say with God, we navigated pretty well. We were able to raise our children with godly principles. My husband owned his own successful electrical business. We pioneered a church that's still thriving today. Bought a couple of houses. So yeah, even with the mistakes, we did great because God was with us and we never gave up. After his passing, my heart was not just broken, but shattered. How to move forward? After we got married, folks would call our names together as one whenever they reached out to us. Instead of Halbert and Rochelle, we became HalbertandRochelle. You never called one without the other.

March 29, 2016, marked a really rough day for me. You see, after my husband's transition in December I had to hold things together. I had to hold it together for my children and for the church we pastored. (Let me tell you those folks loved their Pastor Halbert). Moreover, seeing me fall apart would destroy them. So, I kept it in. There were moments when I was alone, but for the most part, I was all smiles whenever I was around any of these precious people. But on this day, I felt my insides were going to burst. I cried and prayed, seemingly all day and into the night. Finally, that evening I told God I just don't know what to do. I literally said it just like that. Aren't you glad that we can talk to Our Daddy, God, about how we feel and He understands? Some religious folks told me, "Whatever you do, don't let your church see you cry. Be strong. Put on a good face after all your husband is with The Lord, so it's time to rejoice. Let me tell you, that sounded really good, and it was really true. But it didn't stop my heart from feeling like it had broken into a million and one pieces. And for the first time that day, He spoke to me. One thing I have learned over the years is that prayer is not monologue, but dialogue. I speak, God listens and then God speaks, and I listen. Well, I must tell you up until this point, I was doing all the speaking. His question startled me at first but at the same time it was clear and precise. "What do you know?" Then he said, "Write down what you know." This was my list:

1. **I know I love You God.**

2. **I know I miss my husband.**

3. **I know I need time to heal after playing superwoman to everyone.**

4. **I know I must feed myself with The Word of God.**

5. **I know I can't allow myself to get depressed.**

I began to feel a sense of peace all over me as I wrote each (I know) as instructed by The Lord. And just like He always does, He took me to His Word. John 13:1 NLT "Before the Passover celebration, Jesus knew that his hour had come to leave this world and return to His Father. He had loved his disciples during his ministry on earth, and now *He loved them to the very end."* Then The Lord whispered in my ear *"Halbert loved you to the very end."* Oh, what Comfort and Peace those words brought to my soul. At that moment, I knew God understood what I was going through. He knew me and every piece of my shattered heart and soul. I finally went to sleep, smiling because of the assurance of My Lord and Savior. *"He loved me to the very end."* No other words or tears were needed that night. Goodnight my honey. I'll rest in your love tonight.

PRAYER

***Father,** even when we're shattered and torn, we can rely on the fact that You see and understand exactly where we are. Not only that, but You come to our rescue to bring the Comfort and Peace we need to make it to another day. Thank You for being such a Good Daddy-God. Amen!*

Connection Points For Life

My connection point:

He Really Will Wipe Your Tears Away.

Revelation 21:4 NIV

"And God shall wipe away all tears from their eyes; and there shall be no more death, neither sorrow, nor crying, neither shall there be any more pain: for the former things are passed away."

Sometimes a good cry is all you need. It can release accumulated frustrations, worries and cares. And then sometimes a cry can present itself as depression and can be very detrimental for us. Some may call me a crybaby. No matter how many times I've seen Lauryn Hill sing "Joyful, Joyful" on Sister Act 2, I am going to cry. Something about that song touches me deeply when she sings it, and I stopped trying to hold back the tears long ago. Also, when I see those commercials on television about starvation in the land, I just can't help but cry. If it's the right moment and a child gives me a stick as a present, I'm going to cry. Now please understand I'm nobody's wimp, but it's just certain things on the right day that'll start the mighty stream of tears gushing from my eyes. Sometimes I think about my childhood and how many times my mama lacked the finances to provide for us the way she wanted. Although I'm not a wealthy person, The Lord has blessed me to be able to provide for myself. And oh, how I long for my mama to see that I'm okay. She never experienced going on a vacation or owning a car or going shopping at the grocery store without having to put a few items back because she couldn't afford them. I remember the hurtful look on her face whenever she couldn't get an item she needed. Oftentimes, it was a snack of some sort, but unfortunately it wasn't enough on her food stamp voucher to get it. She's with Jesus now and wouldn't trade that for anything in the world. But it doesn't stop me from wishing she was here so I could take her on a vacation. Take her shopping to buy whatever she wants. I think you get the picture. So, I guess I must agree I can be a crybaby, at times.

On this particular day I went to the church to be alone with my tears. It was a few weeks after the death of my husband. That's just the way it is sometimes. On this day my tears were gushing because I was missing my husband. I was so glad no one decided to stop by the church because they may have been frightened of my looks that day. Big puffy eyes, nose and lips. It was a crybaby day. During those times, however, I still prayed, even through my tears. And this day was no different. I began to thank God for loving me despite how I felt abandoned and left alone. I finished my prayer with a continual heart of thanksgiving to My Loving Father and I reached for the tissue box that I had placed next to me when I came in, knowing I would need it. I put the tissue to my face to wipe my tears and there were none. What?!?!?! I knew no one was there with me but still I looked around. Where did the tears go? I checked my clothes, they were drenched with tears, but there were absolutely no tears on my face. I thought, "Wait a minute God, You said You shall wipe away all tears." I can't explain what happened while I was sitting on the front pew of the church that day, but I do believe My Jesus wiped my tears away.

This was such an intimate moment. Everyone has their own thoughts on the word "intimacy," but on that day, I felt so close to God that mere words can't explain . I was able to connect to My Father, My Lord, My Savior, My Everything in a way that I'd never experienced before. I don't know where those tears went but I was glad to have exchanged them for the joy my heart felt at that moment.

You may have never experienced this before, but we all have had those intimate moments with God and God alone. I connected to Him in such a beautiful way. Tell me about yours?

PRAYER

Heavenly Father, *thank you for always knowing where I am and coming to see about me. Although feelings of abandonment, rejection and being alone may happen in our lives we can be assured that You are still there ready and able to bring comfort, peace and tissue when needed. Your loving ways leave us speechless. And for this we say thank you!*

My connection point:

God Owns The "When."

Jeremiah 29:11 NIV

"For I know the plans I have for you," says the Lord. "They are plans for good and not for disaster, to give you a future and a hope."

We weren't able to take many vacations when our children were small. Sometimes we'd get in the car and take a drive to visit family that also lived in North Carolina. And other times, we'd drive over to the next town and get some ice cream, just to give the kids a sense of going somewhere other than school, church and back home again. After riding for just a few moments, one of the kids would ask the question, "When are we going to get there? Or are we there yet?" By the way, that movie was quite indicative of how children ask that question when taking any type of trip. Be it two hours or twenty minutes. My husband and I would both respond with the usual "not yet." For which they would reply "when are we going to get there?" We would try to give an estimate but honestly, we didn't feel compelled to give an answer at all. Our thoughts were, "Be glad we're able to get out of the house albeit for a short period of time and be happy. Geez!"

One thing The Lord taught my husband and I was that He was not bound by time. So, when He gives a promise of a thing, we don't know when He will do it. But we knew it would surely come to pass. As a very young married couple, without a car and with small children, we walked to church. We lived about 2 miles from the church, so it wasn't a big deal. And if I must add, we were always on time. After all, I was the church organist, and my husband was a minister. We were dedicated and faithful to our assignments. Sometimes we would have fasted that day and the summer heat while walking would zap the little energy that we had. Nonetheless, there we were, our little family happily making our way to church. As we walked, we would make up games to amuse the kids, other times we would talk about our hopes and dreams. We'd made a lot of foolish mistakes when we were first married. I don't know why credit card companies send these credit cards to people without finding out if they can be repaid. Believe me when I say it felt so good having that plastic in our wallets and flipping it out to purchase items. It really felt like we were on top of the world. No one really talked about the fact that the bill had to be paid. We were just flipping and spending. When we maxed out one credit card, we applied and received another one. We kept this going until the credit card companies finally figured out that we had no way of repaying those bills and the credit cards stopped. Then we realized this thing called a credit score. I know it sounds funny, but we really had no clue about life and living. We loved each other, got married and began having children without any real plans of how all of this worked. Needless to say, we ended up with a credit score of about 300. We were in bad shape financially. But on those walks, we started the process of disciplining ourselves. We had dreams of being able to provide for our little family and we were determined, with the help of The Lord, to do it. We stopped going to the mall every Saturday on the bus to spend the day getting a warm cookie from the cookie factory. We cooked and ate what we had at home. Be it a pot of beans, a pot of rice or fried chicken. We made do with what we had because we realized that the hole we had dug for ourselves would not just dissolve because we wished it away.

We would conclude our walk to church on those days by encouraging each other. "It won't be this way always and God knows when."

The children of Israel had been taken captive in Psalm 137:1-4 NIV *"By the rivers of Babylon we sat and wept when we remembered Zion. There on the poplars we hung out harps, for there our captors asked us for songs, our tormentors demanded songs of joy; they said, "Sing us one of the songs of Zion!" How can we sing the songs of the Lord while in a foreign land?* These captors were demanding a joyful song after they took them captive. God's chosen knew they would be set free but only God knew *when*. And as we can see, God did what He always does; He restored.

I came across a passage of scripture in Psalm 126:1-6 NIV *"When the LORD restored the fortunes of Zion, we were like those who dreamed. Our mouths were filled with laughter, our tongues with songs of joy. Then it was said among the nations. "The Lord has done great things for them." The Lord has done great things for us, and we are filled with joy. Restore our fortunes, Lord, like streams in the Negev. Those who sow with tears will reap songs of joy. Those who go out weeping, carrying seed to sow, will return with songs of joy, carrying sheaves with them."*

There are times when we go through seasons of weeping. But as my husband and I encouraged ourselves on those long walks to church, say to yourself, "It won't always be this way." You may be going through a season of weeping. As the saying goes "Life Happens." But God has already set aside your *when*. He told the children of Israel, "I allowed you to be drug out of your own land, be shackled like a horse, the men were castrated, and the women were raped. I let you weep as though there was no end. But now I'm going to let you sing again. And those tears were seeds for your harvest."

There are times God will deliver us suddenly, but there are also times when we must go through the process. God owns the *when*! So, I've decided that while I'm waiting on my *when*, I'll trust God for my *win*.

Our stories ended well. We were able to get out of debt, bought a couple of houses and secured our future. It was a process, and the delays were our own mistakes. But I'm so happy that Our God is Faithful.

PRAYER

***Father,** I'm so grateful for your grace and mercies that cover us when we're too foolish to see and do the right thing. Thank you for truly knowing the plans you have for us and bringing them to pass in our lives. You own the when.*

Connection Points For Life

My connection point:

True Victory Starts With Knowing Who You Are.

I Corinthians 15:57 NIV

"But thanks be to God! He gives us the victory through our Lord Jesus Christ."

A person who is confident has certainty about themselves. It's a state of being clear-headed. This scripture is NOT saying we should trust ourselves or even have confidence in ourselves – but it is an assurance of victory through our Lord, Jesus Christ.

Personally, I don't like losing. Anything! Board games, baseball, basketball, words with friends, etc., I'll do what I need to do to win. But just in case I don't actually win you best believe I won't be in last place.

Unfortunately, I wasn't always this way. As a young child I was quite sheltered and very shy. Let me pause right here. If one of my members is reading this, do not laugh. I say that because no one at my church believes I'm a very shy introverted person. Being alone is not a major problem for me. When I stand before God's people, the Holy Spirit is in charge and it's really not me. When I'm done releasing The Word of the Lord, I come back to my shy, introverted self. I can't explain how or why, but it's just part of my makeup.

For one thing, I didn't have much as a child. I wore the same dress to church for about six months. And the reason I stopped wearing it was because I outgrew it. But my mama would send that dress to the cleaners every week to have it cleaned. It was a brown dress with green trim. I was proud to wear it but when I got to church and looked around at my friends, they always had a different outfit. So, I withdrew into a shell. I couldn't express how I felt. And who would I tell? I certainly wasn't going to lay that on my beautiful mama as she was doing the very best she could. So I turned inward with my thoughts and hoped and prayed that I would someday get a new dress for church, too.

Even at school, I was picked on. Bullying didn't just start today. It's been around for decades. By the time I was in the 7th grade, my dear mom had passed away and I was living with my grandmother. We called her Big mama. Big mama lived a pretty modest lifestyle. She'd worked hard in the factory and obtained a little wealth. She and my grandfather bought a beautiful home (two blocks from Berry Gordy). In addition, they bought houses and rented them out for an income. I would say they were doing alright for themselves. For the most part, they were so good to me. They took me shopping and I got to pick out all the clothes I wanted. Boy oh boy. Talk about a candy store experience. By the time I started school in the 7th grade, I already had new outfits that I could wear for at least two weeks. I felt on top of the world. I changed my outer appearance, but I was still a shy, withdrawn child. The bullying didn't stop. I had no clue that I needed to work on how I felt about myself more than looking good and hoping for acceptance. I had so much to learn.

My breakthrough came as I began to grow in the Lord. I looked in the mirror one day and decided I wasn't this ugly person.. I was no beauty queen but neither was I totally unattractive. It's amazing what we believe from others before we look at it for ourselves. That day, when I looked in the mirror, I had an attitude adjustment. I was no longer going to accept what anybody else said about me. That day, I accepted the fact that I was beautiful and it didn't matter who thought otherwise. What a journey. But I was on my way.

So in order to get the full measure of who I was and my purpose for life, of course, I had to go to the scriptures; this is where I turn for answers, encouragement, healing, and relationship problems. You name it. The Word of God has an answer for every single thing we could possibly go through in life.

After discovering that the kids had lied to me about me looking like a dog and me believing it, God began to deal with the inside of me. My soul.

Matthew 10:28-31 NIV *"Do not be afraid of those who kill the body but cannot kill the soul. Rather, be afraid of the One who can destroy both soul and body in hell. Are not two sparrows sold for a penny? Yet not one of them will fall to the ground outside your Father's care. And even the very hairs of your head are all numbered. So don't be afraid; you are worth more than many sparrows."*

Jesus knows me. Jesus cares for me.

Jesus is always with me.

This was my connection point.

John 10:27-29 NIV *"My sheep listen to my voice; I know them, and they follow me. I give them eternal life, and they shall never perish; no one will snatch them out of my hand. My Father, who has given them to me, is greater than all, no one can snatch them out of my Father's hand."*

As I read this my inner man begin to leap.

I am absolutely somebody special. My Daddy, God, is Awesome!

He's my Big God! My protector!

My Shepherd!

And no one can snatch me from Him.

Psalm 8:3-5 NIV *"When I consider your heavens, the work of your fingers, the moon and the stars, which you have set in place, what is mankind that you are mindful of them, human beings that you care for them? You have made them a little lower than the angels and crowned them with glory and honor."*

Talk about an eyeopener.

This passage of scripture lets me see just how much God loved me.

If I had any doubt before it was all gone now.

After meditating on these verses, if you're anything like me, my thoughts about who I was in Christ went up tremendously. In addition to that I thought, how can I be defeated with what I've just heard through the scriptures? I began telling myself how special I was, declaring victory over the different circumstances of life and renewing my mind with God's Word on a daily basis. One thing I have realized is that our mind is the most critical part of spiritual warfare. This is because the enemy is more concerned about what we believe than anything else. So he uses the ammunition of guilt, shame, low self-esteem, loneliness, rejection, etc., to try and keep us under bondage. But The Word says, in John 8:36 NIV *"So if the son sets you free, you will be free indeed."*

Some time ago, I started a game on the computer called Words with Friends. Let me tell you, I was horrible at it. The bad thing was that I was playing against a few people from my ministry. I believe they took great delight in mastering those words. I exited every game feeling defeated. I was getting beat by everybody I knew. That's not a good feeling. With most things in life, I prayed and to me this was no different. I asked The Lord to show me how to come from the back. I mean the way back, and at least be in the same ranks as my church family that was playing with me. A thought came to me to just place the letters that I had on the spaces that would give me the most points. After a few times of trying, I found myself winning. I was no longer just in the ranks. I was winning. Big time! And trust me, I wasn't afraid to brag about it. Now honestly, I had no clue what some of those words meant. But if the game accepted it, that meant it was a viable word. One of my faithful playing members asked me one time what a particular word meant. I told her I didn't know, and I didn't care that I didn't know. But what I did know was that I was winning.

My connection point is that once you realize who you are in Christ, don't accept anything that the enemy has to offer. Even when you feel defeated, don't be satisfied to stay there. Try something else. Change your thoughts. Change your mind. You've already won.

PRAYER

Dear Father, even when I didn't think good things about myself, You did. You knew all along where I would be on my journey with you. And through the different seasons of life, Your love sustained me. Not only that, but You allowed me to hold my head up during every trial knowing You've already planned my victory. I'm so forever thankful and grateful. Amen!

Connection Points For Life

My connection point:

Can Anybody Tell Me How Long Do I Have To Wait?

Isaiah 40:31 NIV

"But those who trust in the Lord will find new strength. They will soar high on wings like eagles. They will run and not grow weary. They will walk and not faint."

Waiting has never been a strong suit of mine. I tend to grow impatient with most things. Pray for me, God's still working on me. But there are times in my life when I absolutely loathe waiting. Traffic lights. Stop signs. Grocery lines. Doctors' office. If someone's picking me up and they say they'll be there at 3:00pm, I start looking for them at 2:45pm. And at 3:01pm I'm pretty much not going to wait any longer. I'll just take myself. I know that's not a good character trait but I told you I'm working on it so please cut me some slack.

I realized this was an issue especially as I've gotten older. I've learned things don't always work according to my schedule. I've also learned things can happen along the way that would cause a person to be late. But most of all, I've submitted that flaw to the Lord for His help and guidance. You do know that when you submit it to God, the test and trials come with that right?

One of these situations happened in the year 1997, the year we bought and moved into our 2nd home. Family was visiting from Detroit and it was Christmas time. I've always been a good cook, at least that's what they tell me. And if I had to put a number on it from 1-10, I'd say I was about an 8 and on occasion possibly a 9. Now understand, I never prepared a large meal for Christmas. Thanksgiving was an entirely different story. You name it, I cooked it. More than likely, our house was filled with folks from everywhere. As they had come to dine at the Richardson's. They knew it would be a spread of the most delectable dishes known to mankind. My famous turkey dressing was normally the star of the show. Everything else was good as well. But this Christmas, with family in town and restaurants closed for the holiday, I had to cook. Well, you know I wasn't going to shortchange my family. After all, they drove all the way to North Carolina to see me. I had to lay it out.

I stayed up late and then got up early to make sure everything was just right. It was my custom to put my turkey on a low heat setting and let it cook all night. The aroma that filled the house made everyone anxious for this meal. We were going to eat until our little hearts were content. But when I got up early the next morning to check on the turkey that had been cooking all night, I noticed there was a leak in the pan it was in, and the oven was smoking a little. Not a lot but enough for me to say, "I better cut this off and grab another pan to finish cooking it." It was then that I discovered I didn't have another pan. What to do, what to do. All the stores that sold that item were now closed. I thought to myself, I knew where I could get a pan. My sister-in-law lived 15 minutes away. However, instead of waiting until the oven cooled down so I could take the turkey out, clean the oven and start fresh with another pan, I made a mad dash to her house to retrieve a pan. Thinking to myself, "I'll get back before anyone wakes up. By the time I get back, the oven will be cooled and I'll finish my Christmas dinner." Now, you did hear me say I should've waited until the oven cooled so I could remove the turkey and clean it right? But impatient Rochelle figured she'd handle it her way, where no waiting was involved. Cleaning it when I returned seemed harmless enough. It'll be cool by that time. The problem was that, although the oven was off, I didn't remove the turkey. With the juice dripping down on the elements, it sparked a fire inside the oven. Do you know how that looked? Well, I'll tell you. It looks as though I started a fire and then left the house. I left the house without informing anyone.

Thank goodness my family from Detroit saw the smoke coming from the kitchen, so they woke everyone up and called the fire department. Everyone got out of the house before my new beautiful kitchen went up in flames.

I got a very calm call from my husband who I guess had deduced that the only place I could be was his sister's house since everywhere else was closed. And he said, "Rochelle, you need to come home." I responded very sweetly thinking that maybe he was just missing his wife. "Okay baby, sure I'm on my way. I'm just sitting here talking to your sister." To which he quickly replied, "No, you need to come now." His voice was a little more emphatic. And he followed that by saying, "The house is on fire." I couldn't comprehend it. I had no idea how, what, where, nothing! I just knew I had to hurry home and hurried I did.

I pulled up to a frantic scene. Fire trucks everywhere. My family was standing outside shivering. I parked on the street and went out searching for my husband. About the time I found him, I saw the firemen dragging my stove out of the house. At that point I didn't need to ask any questions. It was all making sense. And at the core of the questions in my mind, I found the answer. Rochelle! I was the cause.

We eventually joked about that day. But now they were all looking at me very suspiciously. I could hear their thoughts.

"Why did you leave?"

"Where were you?"

"Were you trying to get rid of us?"

"Now what are we going to eat?"

"Do you know it's Christmas and everything's closed?"

All I can say is, "Thank God I lived through that." Even now, at times, my children give me a certain look while telling this story.

And to think none of this would've transpired if I had only waited. I learned a very valuable lesson that day, one that I'll never forget. At times, however, I can become impatient. I want what I think I want, and I want it now. But God has shown me.... Patience is truly a virtue.

Have you ever asked that question, "God what's taking you so long?" If you have, you're in good company because I'm sure millions have asked the same question. But once we truly connect with God, we will come to see and understand why we had to wait.

My word of encouragement to you is that God has not forgotten the promises He made to you. And when you get tired of waiting, learn to lean into Him a little more. He will hold you, sustain you, comfort you and give you peace while you wait.

PRAYER

Dear Father, You created us and know everything about us much better than we know ourselves. We ask you to teach us how to be patient, knowing Your plan is perfect. Help us to know the thing we've prayed and believed you for was truly worth the wait. In Jesus Name. Amen!

Connection Points For Life

My connection point:

Divine Connections

Philippians 1:6 NIV

"Being confident of this, that he who began a good work in you will carry it on to completion until the day of Christ Jesus."

I have no idea where the phrase *'Divine Connection'* comes from. But I have used it for as long as I can remember. To me, it simply means being aligned with God's purpose and plan. It's what we're destined for. And when we are properly aligned with God's purpose it is evident to not only ourselves, but everyone else as well. Simply put...***doing what you know you're supposed to do.***

After the horrific year of 1969 when I experienced the death of my 19 year old brother and 41 year old mom, I went to live with my maternal grandmother. And as I said before, she was the best. She provided me with things in life that I never had. I didn't have to worry about what I was going to eat. Big mama always had plenty of food to go around. And if I happened to not want what she had, she happily took me to White Castle Burgers or McDonald's. Boy oh boy, I was the happiest child ever. I was with the one person I knew loved me and would provide for me. I had my own room. The house was fenced and we had an in-ground swimming pool in the backyard. For the first time in my life, I had a very nice wardrobe of clothes. I didn't have to wear the same dress to church every Sunday. I was happy. But there was something missing. You see, when mama passed away my two brothers, Michael and Jerry, went to live with my father. I never knew life without them. But going to live with my father was the last thing I wanted because our lifestyles were just not the same. Still, I missed my brothers. Mama's gone and now I don't even get to see my two remaining siblings.

To make matters worse, while perhaps I could pass the time by watching a little television, Big mama didn't believe in them and totally refused to bring one into her house. To her, they were a source of devilment. And for as long as I can remember, there was never a television in her home. It wasn't a matter of affordability, she was just convinced that it was of the devil and refused to have any parts of it. Her preference for me was, after completing my homework and chores, turn the radio on to the one and only Jimmy Swaggart and listen to him until the radio signed off. Yes, back in the day, the radio and television signed off at a certain time, unlike now when they can stay on all night long. Well, you have to admit that although I seemingly had every possession in life and was cared for by the most gentle and loving hand of my Big mama, I got bored really quick. A few times, I would go to a girlfriend's house in our neighborhood, but that didn't last either. I contemplated calling my father to say pick me up, but I knew that would absolutely not be the answer.

My cousin, Richard, had connected with a Pastor from North Carolina. He was conducting a revival at Mattie Moss Clark's husband's church. His name was Elder Curtis Cole. He was an awesome teacher and preacher of God's Word. He had a connection with young people even though he was older. People from all over the United States flocked to North Carolina to be under his tutelage. When my cousin Richard accepted Jesus as Lord of His life, he went full steam ahead. We went to the same school and I would find him going up and down the hallways telling our high school students about Jesus Christ. He had absolutely no shame about his walk with The Lord. Some would accept his words, others would heckle him, and some others would ignore him completely. But he never stopped. He would move over to the other hallway with a smile and invite them to say yes to Christ.

At some point Richard desired to move to North Carolina to be mentored by Elder Cole. Let me tell you I loved The Lord but at the time, I was never as enthused as Richard. I wanted acceptance with the cool kids and all of this Jesus talk was cramping my style. Today, I guess I would be considered a Sunday morning church girl. Nevertheless, I truly did love The Lord. I just wasn't as aggressive as my cousin Richard.

One summer, he returned from North Carolina to visit us back home in Detroit. He began telling me about all the young people at the church there and how they interacted with one another on a daily basis. They traveled together, went to dinner with each other and everything. He made it very exciting. So, the next summer, I decided that I would go to North Carolina to see exactly what he was talking about. My grandmother agreed, purchased my airline ticket and off I went. Let me tell you, it was everything he said it was. Everyone was so nice and friendly. The young people were just as eager as Richard to spread the gospel of Jesus too. This was very new to me.

I enjoyed my summer there, especially as I got to play the organ. Now I wasn't a skilled musician, but I loved music and the organ was at the top of the list. And because the church was smaller than my church in Detroit, they allowed me to practice on them. At first, I was absolutely terrible. But I began to put time into practicing and over time I got a little better. I guess you can say I did okay for myself in that area. I became the minister of music for my local church in Winston Salem, the district minister of music and eventually the state minister of music.

But after my summer, I trekked back home to Detroit. But somehow, I knew life in Detroit would never be the same. I felt such a divine connection in Winston Salem, North Carolina. There was a longing in my heart that said, *'that is where you belong.'* At the time, I was happy to spend every summer in NC. But the next summer when I arrived, I stayed a little longer, so much so that school was starting here in NC. And Elder and Mother Cole suggested that I go since everyone else would be in school so I did. A week went by, another week went by, then another. After a while, Elder and Mother Cole asked me, "Do you want to stay here?" To which I quickly replied, "Yes!" I'm not exactly sure what arrangements they made with my grandmother. All I knew was that after a few phone calls, they told me that Big mama consented to me staying.

It was my **Divine Connection**. I met and married and had my children here, and also continued ministry here. Along with my husband, we founded a church here. Became a grandmother here, and a spiritual mother to too many to count.

I would say, without a doubt, I'm exactly where I am supposed to be.

What about you? Have you ever known without any shadow of doubt that you were to embark upon a thing? Connect with a person? All I can say is that I am so grateful to our Lord Jesus Christ for His perfect plan for my life.

One of my favorite scriptures is Acts 17:28 NIV *"For in Him we live and move and have our being."* Tell me about your Divine Connection.

PRAYER

Father, we are learning daily what it truly means to trust you. We would have long made a terrible mess of our lives. Thank you for being our guide, our hope, our future and our right now. We are especially thankful for connecting us with those who would bring purpose to us. Help us to always know that You have the best plan for us. And although it may seem strange or different, give us the peace and faith to obey. In Jesus Name. Amen!

My connection point: